Body. Voice. Mind. Mouth.

POEMS BY

LOUISE ROBERTSON

Brick Cave Media
brickcavebooks.com

Body. Voice. Mind. Mouth.

Cover Illustration Artist: Bob Tavani

Brick Cave Media
brickcavebooks.com
2025

For Bob Tavani and Joan Robertson
None of this would have happened without you

Body. Voice. Mind. Mouth.

POEMS BY

LOUISE ROBERTSON

Brick Cave Media
brickcavebooks.com

Contents

V. Refrain

I. Body

The Apple Diet, A Timeline

The baby food diet son of
the maple syrup diet son of
the raw foods diet son of
juice fasting son of
the Atkins diet son of
the Scarsdale diet son of
the Beverly Hills diet son of
the grapefruit diet son of
the Cabbage Soup diet
son of the cigarette diet
son of Graham's diet son of
the vinegar and water diet
and on back in time
to the apple diet.
And God lied:
Thou shall not eat of it, neither shall thou touch it
thou shall not tongue its shiny skin,
do not slip it into thy body,
do not let it travel through thee,
do not nourish thyself,
do not feed it to thyself,
do not feed lest thou die. But rather
than death be shunned by food,
weight, and size, do this while thou birth children
in pain and so begat
my line.

And Eve begat Tantalus and
Persephone and the fasting girls
and Karen Carpenter
and Jane Fonda
and on down to my grandmother and
my mother and there —
in the yellow-floor kitchen
with the vertical, harvest gold refrigerator
with loaves of bread on top

with gleaming red fruit in a stemmed
green glass bowl on the table
with vines and gourds running through
the bright wallpaper —
there, that's where I was born. In that garden.
Sssssss.

Canvas

Take your canvas to
the coffee shop. Sit that canvas
on the chair. Pour hot chocolate
into its mouth. Like a kiss.
Like a kiss.

Celery

I hate that my name means love. I hate
that my name, when written or spoken,
means I have to say "love" to you, to everyone.
It's embarrassing. When

you flash your bleached teeth at me,
I don't want to love you. When you
simper and whine and jerk
yourself back and forth, anxious

as a weed on a highway, I don't want to love you.
My parents did this to me. How could
they know that it feels like I am
Superman when I love someone

except that, instead of opening
my shirt to reveal a bright S, when
I open my ribs – like the wings
of a jacket – my lungs and

pancreas fall out. I hate that.
I don't want to please you. I don't
want to teach you anything. I
do not want to do as my mother did

when she peeled off the cardboard
outsides of the celery,
pulled off the strings
and fiber, and worked out

the soft inside stem,
held it up for me.
It's the best part she said,
and then she gave it away.

Not the Whole Story

She lost the baby and her
uterus on the same
day. I think she thought

life was supposed to have been
a forced march from then on,
full of kerosene and stethoscopes.

Did someone tell her she could
only wash in two minute showers? Because
that's what she did. Did someone tell

her to be thrifty only with herself?
Because that's what she did. Still,
she was a queen

on the living room couch,
plush chickens for dinner
and all the kids she could adopt.

II. Voice

Fried Chicken, 1981

Joanie props her elbows on the table cloth
then picks up a chicken leg-
and-thigh combo, dredges
it through egg and milk, through
breadcrumbs with flecks
of green and black, nestles it
in with the rest of the body. Later, Joanie
hunches over stove and frying pan,
before pushing the tray
into the oven for, oh,
35 minutes, and back to the table
with her elbows
pointer finger,
still unbent by time,
aimed to the ceiling
to mark her words,
and she looks out the window
where we will never build
an addition. This is the process
no one else seems to use
to get their chicken fried
and I know
other people's recipes
are supposed to be good,
but hers is the greasiest cracked
pepper and salt
love I have ever tasted.

People Whose Mothers Leave through the Door of Alzheimer's
(If only the Rapture had taken her)

My mother is not leaving through the door of Alzheimer's.
Her sister did. Her father did. Her father's
sisters and brother did. Years ago,
while her sister
was floating in it (early, early), memories sinking to the bottom
of the pool (as it were), while her dad was
stumbling into it, teeth first, wincing,
it was her own private rapture. Now
she gets to say everything she should have
years ago. She gets to push her feet
into cold sand and watch the storm roll in
over the beach and be fully aware of where she is,
and who is there
and who isn't
and why.

To the Ball Python Who Lived in Our Dining Room

Sweetheart, you too were a chapel,
nosing your glass box at dusk, peering

from behind plastic leaves
at dinnertime.

Your sunsets peeked through curtains;
your breezes wafted from the screen

ceiling. Raccoons visited your bay
window leaving muddy handprints.

Who prey? Who predator?
We thought of calling an ambulance.

We googled your demise.
We rued the many dead mice on offer

when live ones were not
available. And your rigor

mortis stiffened you next to the milk.
What lenses you have to view us

from the sidebar, from the interior
of our refrigerator turned morgue,

from the maple tree's roots and
mounds of grainy soil?

Sins like ours
don't get to a priest. But you hallow

our ground, beloved.
Forgive us.

Tech Cycles

I spent today — the morning, the afternoon —
wired up, connected,
fingertips to keyboard, practically

two tech cycles away
from a chip in my head.
Then late in the day, while explaining

email tracking codes
to a silk-scarf, a stain of sunshine
spilled in through glass block,

kissing my hands, fogging the zoom
with a memory of the white station wagon
we used to take to church and back home,

its red carpet and vinyl interior bleeding on itself
from rainwater and gaps in the frame.
That doesn't happen anymore.

The bench seats, the hard plastic, dad's
nicotine glazing the insides of the windows brown.
But mornings, afternoons,

I am wired up, connected,
practically a chip in my head,
complete with a thousand

polymer threads to link neurons
to keyboard, but late
I explain, there's silk, rain,

a spiderweb loose in the forest, glassy,
collecting what doesn't happen anymore,
shiny, tracking,

it's code, the stain on the windows,
fog, home, vinyl, link,
my parents, the metal

memory and zoom, ruby mornings, red nighttimes,
a leak in the frame,
seat belt shoved between stiff cushions.

I spent today, we, the sun, a kiss
bleeding in my hands,
back home, memory spilled,

I could feel the forest, a web,
its DNA, a glaze, summer in February,
all this dreaming and un-dreaming

practically a chip in my head.

My Manic Bitch

There's no point to
owning a fence. My bitch
chews under it, manic
for a possum. There's
no point to the cross
beams reinforcing the fence,
my bitch parkours
to the top to get at
a deer, her mud tracks
spattered up the planks of wood.
There's no point to a leash, either,
when another dog passes.
My bitch bites the neck
of the strap and wrestles me.

Sure, she lies in the sun,
a quiet bitch next to my beach chair,
or gnaws (but gentle)
on my fingers. She must dream
of the jump that crests the fence,
or the tug that makes me drop the lead.
And maybe we both imagine that —
her stretching
in a dead run across the neighborhood,
terrifying and glorious.
Why the fence? Why the fence?

You Would Hate Me

if you heard me sing. All
my sins show up. How I
hesitate to say the right words.
How I pretend to be a soprano.
I can hear it doing harm
to your good ears by trying too hard.
How flat I am. What a pretender.

I sing to myself
a little, though.
Talk to myself, too. Will do
all the way to blackness
when I shut down,
teeth loose, armor tarnished.

Climate Change Elegy

Safe Ohio. Easy
Ohio. Green Ohio.
Tropical Ohio. Soft
Ohio.
Before it was Ohio
Ohio. People traveled
through here Ohio.
Beavers big as
Volkswagens Ohio.
Used to be 90 percent
forest Ohio. There should be more
moths Ohio. Where
are the butterflies Ohio.
This is too safe
Ohio. This is too easy Ohio.
This is too green,
soft, tropical, driven,
empty, crowded,
growing Ohio. Used to it Ohio.
Ohio, Ohio. Will be
used-to-
be Ohio.

On the Inadvisability of Good Decisions

I regret my good decisions while
staring at digital timestamps within
the carpeted walls
of my assigned cubicle as November
darkens to evening right after lunch.
I regret them as I climb
into the hybrid and track its mileage.
On an after-work walk,
plastic bags, candy wrappers, and
beer cans sprawl.
I decide to corral
strips of wild sheeting
massed into a wig of see-through hair.
A slippery ooze
crawls onto my hands.

I should have fucked that guy.
I should have broken my heart
over him and kept breaking those gears
— a clockwork that spends almost
all of its time junked
just for those
two moments everyday,
when it is exactly right.

The Onerous Duty of Reading a Daily Poem Sent by Email

It spawns at seven am,
slides into the inbox, at
7:01. Haiku

for a title, some
reference to childhood
or trees or breeze or

trauma and I pause
before unrolling the thing, knowing
— we are all experts in digital surveillance —

my click is counted,
reading time tracked. A/B
testing likely applied. To unsub

is to send a frown. To report as spam
is to reject with a fuck-you.
This poem could be joyous,

I coach myself. The first
line is a promise or
a little dull.

I could delete, but
it's open now and
gusts its emo dawn:

words written with light.
I bow over my phone and
give it its tax and

it deploys its brief
symphony of sentiment,
its curling and hot

imaginary wind.

Divorce

First, protect yourself. Don't nurse
the squirrel with eyedropper, skin, and salt,
but with the darkness
of a punctured shoebox. Do
not cuddle him with your body.
Leave the animal alone.
Your noises
are wrong for him.
You confuse him. You prolong
his suffering and his death. He will
linger under your guidance,
not to mention the languages you're
stilling in his heart, not to mention
the languages stilling
in your heart.

To Those Who Precede Us
Written for Gina Blaurock, again, March 2024

Crocus mouths open up.
Plates of water simmer on the road.
Magnolia trees pin on their widest
yawns. Every year, it's like this.
It'll be like this next year. I'll write
almost exactly the same thing.
Teeth-colored clouds grind
against each other. Maples pop
their bloody, ticklish flowers. No you.
No us. I this. I that.
Sun piles up in my hands
like I'm the luckiest bastard ever.

Re-Piercing My Mother's Ears: the Plan,
written in conversation with and Play's program Open Fields

The plan is to lay my mother
 in her easy chair
and soap her earlobe
with warm water
while Frank Sinatra sings
from the iPhone.
First, we will joke around
about the steel pin in my hand
and jump scares. I will
not get her back for playing
"pinch crab" on beach vacations
with her little daughters.
How could she be so mean! I thought
at the time from my small life where
I had not yet had someone who loved me
hurt me. But the plan for next week,
requires calm. I will recall
those very same beach vacations
to her, with the slippery tides,
the tin foil water, the creak
of metal chairs whose rounded bars
pushed into sand bumps
with our weight. I will have her
imagine bobbing on the waves
on a rubber raft, people distant, cold
shivers below, a few drifting
jellyfish, a boat spreading waves
from two acres away.

Then I will ease the pin
through her half-closed piercing
moving from back to front
and I will recall my own child
who wondered if it really hurt me
when she stepped on sidewalk cracks

and so she stepped
on the sidewalk cracks just to see
what would happen.

The Family Kingdom

As long as my mom can sit
at her table, the plane of her face
tilting sideways like this is a secret,

as long as the fluorescent light torches
her skin with white, as long as the spots
on her arm make an ivy of freckles,

as long as the yard outside darkens
with sticks, as long as the linoleum
is pimpled with dirt,

she will reign.

Made or Just Happened

We are up to our eyeballs in the debate:
Are we temporary or recycled
or transitional or
vinegar or salt water or
iron train rails or waves
or ripples or puddles
or now or later
or sometimes.
I am
one of the discarded.
I am one of the loved.
I am one of the eyeballs
in the debate and no one
believes me but here we are:
arguing.

Water

There's been so much rain that all week a braid of water has slid down the gutter, rushing for the sewer, creek, and rivers. It meshed with itself like a few of the trees in my backyard; two Bartlett pears and a maple have twined up with each other. That's what we look like sometimes: one minute we are toe to toe, the next it's not clear whose limb is where and we are trying to merge. Here I want to add "but that's ok, we were lonely for a long time" as if loneliness were the price of the stage I have made with this poem. We feel compelled to lead with our trauma; it grants an authority. We get so bored of our traumas. We never want to talk about the car accident again; We never want to say I am broken again. I'd rather be one of the people who feels like the trees in my backyard, like rain water in the gutter, feet in the damp soil, a stretch, a lengthening, somehow mixed up with air, ground, and sunlight.

When Did You Focus So Much Everything Else Fell Away?

Yesterday. Right now. Last night.
The lightning and its trailing
thunder beat at the windows. We were
at the center of the storm,
one of us sleeping, one of us about
to be sleeping. All the time. Again.
Silk. Flash. Buzz. Darkness.

Re-Piercing My Mother's Ears: The Actuality

Her ear, dough-soft, yielded
to the awl of the earring
because she is so

like me, my ears are pliant like
that, stretched
bread.

We laughed the whole time
— me, my sister, and her.
First we positioned our mother

for the deed. Then we
took turns with the prong
starting from the back

and pushing through a little, then trying
from the front.
Buckets of blood were mentioned

and childhood grievances.
And here's where my memory
of the punch bothers me:

it was hard to hurt her.
I've pierced
myself plenty, but

I couldn't do it to her.
I couldn't do it to her
and then, I could.

In Which I Visit Bertrand Russell and Epicurus and Philippa Foot

My descendants fear death
even when I tell them they won't be there
to feel it. Especially then.
And the ocean rinses your feet.
And the rain spits on the car roof.
My descendants insist they will take care of me
in my old age even when I tell them
to leave me alone. Especially then.
And the pavement heats the air like the air is meat.
And the lake water cooks grasses in the summer.
Them and me: we can't hear each other too
well. Nightly, I visit my friends in hell
in the form of books who don't
worship hell and wake in the morning,
singed eyebrows smelling of the different ozone
of that afterlife. Parents
show you how they want to be treated.
So I mailed letters for my father
and took my mom to the beach.
For the tide, for the hot sand,
for the way everything is everything is everything.

loved.

"You know, Hafiz was outrageous. He said if the beloved tells you to drink poison, you drink poison." - Timothy Liu

I think most of my beloveds have wanted to
tell me to drink poison

many times over, as most of them
discovered I didn't belove them as they liked

or rather I wasn't doing what they thought a belover should do
or rather I wasn't the belover they imagined me to be

and they really beloved that idea of me. So
there I would have been, had they asked, lips blue

with belovement, muttering,
shivering, muttering, "I did belove you."

But we both would have known I'd done it wrong
and in fact was just pretending to drink the poison.

Proof: I never ate the rotten potato at least one of them
actually prepared for me. I couldn't even

belove them like a great poet. Look at all the wasted
words I'm not supposed to use.

It's like the beloving I didn't do the way I was supposed to.
Beloved, you are such a wasteland, I'd say,

and they wouldn't understand at all.
I do nothing right. Not poems. Not belovement. And yet I know,

I know, I beloved them. I especially beloved
the one who would never have me drink poison,

who would have pushed that cup aside
and suggested we swill coffee instead and we'd laugh

at ourselves, so fat, so alive, so

My Mother's Breasts

My mother checks her pocket,
the one snapped to her
bra. She slithers in, her hand
pursed like a kiss, and bites off a wad
of cash. We worship her
too salty skin. We adore
the blazing smile. But

we fear the rack.
We mock it,
slapping our arm
on the restaurant table like
her heavy breasts. We would
never be like this, we think.
We would never succumb
like that. We hatchlings, we
snakelets, have nothing to do
with the weight of gravity. We

burrow against the body. We lean
around it. We tether ourselves to it
when we want to brave a cliff of wind,
then go dancing away,
starving ourselves, singing
about all the wealth of the world,
starving, singing, starving.

She Looks Bored, You Say, of the Dog

And, yeah, she is a veritable ode
to summertime, languishing,
unbothered by copters mixing the sky,
barely twitching when the mail
comes. Heat happens differently to dogs:

tongues lap the air,
while we glaze ourselves. But
is it wrong of me to
think of that other heat
we denied her? The swell,
the seeking, a pull on the nipples?

She would have had beautiful puppies,
red brown, black eyebrows, expressions
like a question, a paw
on our arm often. We hold
hands at the vet's.
Is this her contained
yearning and our
mistake to see all this lying
around on couches as ennui?

I keep my opinions to myself
this time, having had it all.
Still I shiver
when air shuffles through yellow grass,
hose water snakes in the dry earth,
and I hear a child yelling, "Mama."

After

She gave me the bottle
from the beach house
after the place sold
after it flooded
after we spent all those
summers there with the ocean
breathing next to us
often frying
baloney and nightly holding the Old Bay
in our noses like a sneeze
while we shivved
crabs apart after salt
grass
after muck
walking in the gray mornings
on the Chesapeake side for clams
mildew and stilled air fuming
among the reeds
after sun screen and Noxema
smeared on hot skin
and spending the day and night
with fake coconut and menthol
mixed after she couldn't walk
the half block to the sand anymore
but we drank wine and played
poker and canasta and liar's
dice all day with
softened cards and several
different sizes of dice —
I snapped open the lid
of the shampoo
and there was my mother,
her hair
kind of frizzy
in the sea air.

III. Mind

I Wasn't Prepared For Anything

Even if you had told me to mind
the boys who pushed up on me —
I felt unprepared to push back.
Men actually touched me
in elevators and subways
and I made up nicknames
for their plausible deniability attacks,
their escape hatch tears. How nice
they thought they were to invite themselves over
and expect everything and say nothing.

Even if you had told me to study hard
at college, I was cool
instead, having learned to
appear unruffled by advances.
The chill breezes! Emulated and avoided.
Certainly I wore black, melted
myself to 92 pounds, endured
my misguided romantic attachments
and detachments.

Even if you had told me you
would depart — just slump over at lunch —
I wouldn't have believed you.
We were planning Thanksgiving!
We were discussing who wore what
at Katie's wedding.
And if in a passing comment you would
note that you liked me, thought I was cool,
I'd have overlooked its importance:
a bunch of yellow roses, pink lipstick
and blue carpet turning into powder
under our feet.

Twins

They ask, of the two of us,
who will die first or
whether I would like to die
before she does. We do everything
five minutes apart.
Birth, names, cars.
One then the other.
We grew that way
— an inch up, then the other
an inch over that — until I woke one day,
five inches taller than she was
— alone, just like that. It took
six years for her to catch up.
Me the dog with three legs, the goat
in the rocks, a shy goose.

Of course,
I want to outlive her, get
the last word in. I had a five-
minute, five-inch lead and I still want to win.
She will never forgive me for the legs,
the rocks, or the holler of the goose.

Heaven and Earth

Her heaven requires you believe
in it to get there. It requires confession
of sins. Submission to a ladder
of authority.

My sister can meet her there.
I will remain here, sparrows
landing their feet in dirt that was my face,
my old consciousness a dimming lamppost
snapped off in the night.

Her earth was girdled by her faith.
But none of it seemed real to me,
not the way feathers, iron, and concrete
are real. I've heard it said,

we are earth. And ashes to ashes
is the only part of the ceremony
I thought I could nod my head to.

Snake Handler

My brother said suicide is a trap door.
I think it's also like that snake he owned.
If I kept a snake like that,
it would stay still most of the time,
there in its terrarium, hot lamp
on warm rock. A coil.
A braid. Sometimes I would
drape it on my body. Let it
shiv my back. A shotgun. A rope.
The whole time venom collects
in its teeth. He teases me with that
thought. About the suicide door. That snake's mouth.
How it might spring open and shut.

Sorry

I say sorry like
it's a blanket or painted mask.
A dodge, a bright hot wire. It's
my largest muscle and my fashion sense. Prayer
and penance both. Flagellation.

That is, until she said —
when I nearly bumped into her (saying sorry) —
she said, "You're fine."
Like I needed her permission.

What does she know of my sins, buried
as they are in sugar and manners,
a garden of kneeling and cringe.

I can lie to myself so hard,
it makes me stand up straight
in a grocery store aisle
like I belong there.

My sins are a giant
with stiff fingers, broken,
warmed by constant use. That giant
can hold your hand, look in your wet, wet eyes
and make you back down. Sorry.
I am that giant. Sorry.

I have made a meal of sloth and a nest of gluttony
and a eulogy of curses. But lust, sorry, lust
is my ark.

And that lady says, "You're fine."
My ship of transgressions lists in the bay of my ever-growing
days — the water, a soft bed for all I've committed.
That lady has no idea what the hell I'm sorry
for. I'm fine?
Fuck fine. Can't you hear me?
I'm sorry.

Her Clear Mind

When my dad died, it was a relief
to no longer hear him breathe
like a hollow log, drowsing.

When my grandmother
died, it was after she'd already sailed
her ship away. Her body fiddled for years

with no song except the wind
playing across the strings. My grandpop
and his $100 bills slipped away, too,

before the lights fully drained out. So I
have no map for processing the loss
of a woman, awake till the end,

a muscle, a pitchfork, a good laugh stopped.

Sand Fills Everyone's Mouth

I'm supposed to worship you now,
aren't I? But death mutes a god,
puts razor wire around

the statue. It lets your stone feet
sink into mud, lets your words
scald the beach

and wash away.

The Count Is Now 2 and Whatever

2 being the number
of people whose feelings I hurt
I mean the last thing I did
I mean the last thing I did to them
was I hurt their feelings
and I have the text messages to prove it
it feels like I am Peter
— deny deny deny — like that
and it feels like if I were Jesus
and my friends denied me
well if I were Jesus I would know
that cowardice is how
Peter survived the day and if I were
Jesus I would think my friend Peter
should survive the day and if denying
me was what did it then ok deny
I told my daughter to do that to blame
me to say my mom is such a bitch
I have to go home she won't like me drinking
and then I taught her to pass the joint to the next person
if that's what she wanted
she had my blessing
my parental blessing and I am no Jesus
she had my blessing to kick me in the head
metaphorically
if she had to and I let her know ahead of time
so she didn't have to pause
I said blame me say what a bitch say that
and I heard her do it once
so proud
and so if my friends are denying me that's fine
I think if I am hurting
my friends like that I think
they would forgive me
like Jesus and if they wouldn't
then we hurt each other and that is how
they left the world in pain and me too
I'm in pain too
they are gone and I hurt them.

Ant

She must have been living
on the mat for weeks, fat on
crumbs, sugar, loneliness. Like
a scatter, she scrambles over a knee. Later
she appears on the dash, then on the side
window. Such a big, round
abdomen, shell rubbed and dulled by
the dark afternoon. Will
you be my Wilson, stranded by this
commute, ant? Will you be
a madeleine or lanyard?
A genie's bottle, more like.
A place to put complaints
described as wishes
and so we drive home — wishing
complaining, wishing.

Fucking Beautiful

She came to the show after a workout
telling me the weight range she wanted to be
I said nothing because it was
the weight range I am already
and I want to lose 20 pounds
so I said that — I want to lose 20 pounds
but I was supposed to say you're so slender and
you don't need to lose weight
— which she didn't need to — but I caught
myself because people say stuff
like that so disingenuously
she would think I didn't mean it
so I said nothing except
that stupid lose-20-pounds-myself
comment which is true but
beside the point
I didn't want
her to think me disingenuous
but she is so fucking

beautiful — is my mouth open —
her current weight
range equals fucking beautiful
and her current body is exactly right
for those clothes and
I think maybe I told
her about a dream — why — in which
my clothes fit but
the scale said 120 pounds
more than usual and somehow
in the dream I just
shrugged — like who gets
on the scale sees +120
and shrugs but that's what
I did and I wanted to tell
her — you fit your

clothes and fit
clothes fucking beautifully and
your current body equals
exactly right like who does
that but you should do
that my young friend you
weigh body equals
fucking beautiful.

Train Song

Stand there
nose two feet away from
its rush and the rubbed silver

tracks and clacking
grooved wheels chorus are lure and warning.
Wake in the night, as its blast

free styles — a 22 mm bullet
of whatever you're worried about
in your skull.

Chest
clench as the bully noise
pushes people and cars forward.

At its station, the squeal
brake of power pauses.
We made this species,

these robotic
offerings that rush
through countryside

and grime: the coo,
the call, the trill, the warble,
the hoot—caw, caw.

Objects of Study: Our Bodies

mirror desert igneous
rock lion boot
muscle worn built pulse
that fist-shaped bird
tattooing ribs from the inside
cat-quick a flick steeled
— we remember Osiris
and Jesus too both of us
die and rise
on this bed.

Diminuendo al Niente

For years, my religious brother has stuffed his depression
diagnoses into his pockets. Now he starves himself,
becomes gaunt as a plank.

"I weigh 107 pounds," he says.
My brother likes the ceremony of the church
as if it were both a hot wire puncture

and the white dressing around it. Even so,
no holy oil spread on his face seems to help.
He ignores the doctors, too.

What can I say to him? As soon as a priest laid hands
on me, I went and knelt before the altar
of the written word. I text him mornings, trying to avoid the sin

of telling him how much I enjoy the salt and fish of the world.
Otherwise, he'll say how he wishes he could have that.
The only answer I have is no answer:

Look, brother, look at the blocked bodies
of the concrete river locks soaking in the water.
You could make a nave of those repeating forms

fading into the fog and make incense
of their murk and mark the high tide lines.
You could make a prayer of that. You could.

Dear Second Love

The black and yellow heart of the tulip
has peeled itself

in the sun,
made of itself an eaten orange.

That's us.
Already open.

Benediction for a Cup of Coffee

First, open the mouth
of the kettle so it can swallow
a belly of tap water. Put that on
the warming stove, then salt
the French press
with a thick tablespoon of
ground coffee, but sift a flat
teaspoon of sugar into a mug.
Spill boiling water into the French press,
and milk into the cup. Then,
you pray. Or rather, don't pray,
study the backyard, simmering
under a fresh snow – its duvet,
its compress, its damp sweater.
Or maybe, in the dark kitchen,
use your feet to accept the cold floor.
If only church had this kind of
eucharist, a sensation I could think
about and hate and love,
and feel thankful for. Oh my god,
chill on the skin, on the distal phalanges,
the proximal metatarsals and what
is that vibration coming from the house,
its foundation, and
the earth beneath like yet another
burning sunrise?

Grief as a Road

Most people who have stood on this road,
looking around with a wing of sunlight

glassing their eyes tell me what to expect.
It's all true like bone turned into pearls.

Doesn't hurt any less to run into a brick
wall when you are told "You're going to run into a brick wall."

Or it does. Or it doesn't. Again. And again.

Ode to Popcorn

After I wrote the poem
about my mother's fried chicken,

I read it to an Upper Arlington crowd
someone asked for the recipe.

Didn't you hear the poem, I said—
or didn't say because come on, it's right there.

That's how I feel about the word popcorn;
the cracked hulls and hot moisture, the big bang

writ small. Sop it in oil, sprinkle it
with seasoning. Salt. Butter. Pepper.

Cumin will have me sniffing my coated
fingers for hours. How greedy. Nutritional

yeast for the robust members of our tribe.
My family agrees, if you can't share,

make another batch. Use the dutch oven; re-fill
the big green bowl, the one bought for

this purpose, to reduce conflict, cause
fewer simmering wars, make enough for breakfast,

a snack with lunch, something to hide in the fridge.

On the Delicate Task of Making a Password

Passwords are eyelashes. Or
fortune cookies. Or crickets.
Some people use the same one
over and over, like entering
the name of that guy,
but spelling it wrong.
Some people make
selfies out of them.
You should be afraid of them,
how they tell on you, how
they make plain your wishes,
how they rattle in your cochlea,
that thing you meant to
say, but never did. You
should be so lucky when
it turns out to be a child's
name, a birthday, a thing
you made into breath
and water, the sweat dripping
into the ribbed cave of your ear
like a song.

Self-Actualization

The earth
invented us

to inhale the water
shuffling along a gutter or

sinking into the grass.
It wanted to absorb its scent

steaming from its loam.
It wanted to sense the squirrel

eyeballing the leaf, the flat flounder
as she flutters into pliant silt

at the bottom of the bay, the leech
inserting a proboscis into

the mouth of her prey, and the prey
receiving that eucharist.

Even the guinea worm
knows something about our skin

that we do not as she gnaws
her way through our feet

to make more guinea worms
in the drinking water.

The different view
is the point, might

be the argument forwarded
by the cancer

in the eyes of the Tasmanian
Devil as she jumps

from one pup to another.
A pigeon scraping her claw

on a concrete curb experiences
the grain of that texture differently

than scuffed cow
leather would.

So many mediations
on earth, by earth.

So many ways to sense
a breeze simpering its

way along the surfaces of
a wet or drying

slug. Cannot this whole place be
one act of self-love? Won't it be

a pleasure to announce
every sensation as holy

in the way that love
is always holy?

Some throats know
the shape of a scalpel

when they talk. It's there
anyway, whether or not

we say the words, but
we do often feel compelled to say

the words, don't we
as we listen to

each other tell on ourselves, hear
the authority of our lived

knowledge: what quick blades,
what slick wounds.

The earth can
devour us so easily: a tide,

a wind, a plume of poison.
It calls us home

and we go.

IV. Mouth

After the Post about the Death of a Classmate Appears

The impulse to remember
the one bad thing he did
is strong here.

But I owl at his last Facebook image,
his left cheek more like a sink, his bald eyes
have seen the thing

we joke about on Halloween.
His skin a marsh. So I set
aside whatever I thought of him

DM'ing me while
posting happy-birthday-lovely-wife
messages. I know he almost

died in our 3rd grade classroom.
Crumbs of a life
out here, online.

And my mother
just laid out too.
I remind everyone

in an effort to teach
myself: what I say of her
I must say of him.

It was complicated.
She lived. Was lucky.
Wasn't.

America

Joy, like a car, teaches
you nothing, or rather
it teaches
you to keep doing the same thing,
Over and over.

Do this.
Refill this.

Pay
anything to feed this
to bursting.

When gasoline smells, you
keep on huffing.
How hot it gets in that thing
and you stay there,
hoping it's the kind of fire
you can put in your mouth
and it won't hurt you.
I mean like a cigarette. I mean like a gun.

The Kidney

I would give up a kidney
for my sister faster than
call her on the phone. I'd give
her a kidney instead of
listening to her tell me
I'm going to hell. I'd give up
a kidney and enjoy the thought
of my flesh working in her
body — the body so like
my body — the body so
unlike my body. I've been
saying for years
I'd give her a kidney.
I never thought I'd have
to do it. I'd give up a kidney
for her so she could get
rid of that shriveled stone
she's been carrying around
since we were toddlers.
I'd give up a kidney
and refuse to hear a thank you.
Pass, I'd say. Enjoy it, I'd say.
We could share a drink
— a light drink. I could
make that happen.
She would remind
me to see the best in people
and I would remind her
to see people for who
they are. We'd both get mad.
She'd say I'm going to hell. I'd agree
that she's being a bitch.
We'd be different like twins are different:
the pair of us,
running around
completely separate.

Binging

Well   thank god
we use the word

to mean something
else   now   it's

          clean   cozy
                   no drains, no

ass buckets with faces in them
                              white mirror /

black mirror.
This is righteous swallowing, ingestion

                        no shivering with tile lines impressed
          on your knees /
          teeth scars on your knuckles

          premature atrial contractions convulsing

My Mother's Highest Goal

I'm not sure I know what to do
with myself now that there's

no one to think I shouldn't
do what I want or be what I want

or go where I want. I feel
anonymous now that there's

no phone call waiting for me
to suggest a more discrete life,

a cat in the window might be
a good role model for me.

I am not sure if I should have been more ordinary
or less.

The Garden of Earthly Delights

In this bed, we are in the garden
of earthly delights. I am the garden
of earthly delights with you, also the garden of
earthly delights surrounded by the walls, which
define this garden of earthly delights, in which
we have the kneeling floor and the fall over
pillows. The middle panel of life, here,
and so we pray: Oh my Hieronymus Bosch,
we are heartily living. You and I
could be anyone doing this dance and
lucky for me this I mean here it is I you we
being the garden delights earth.
It's made every morning
every night. And the next day: we feast again.

The Cat's Love Song

The cat's claw massage
is his love song. His sweater chewing,
also love. His damp fur ball.
His perch on the hip while
reading. I rotate and he shifts his heft,
staying on top of rock mountain body.
The jump from bed to window. The pallet
made of my stomach. The stare. The rattle.
The swipe at a jewelry box holding mom's
diamond earrings — the swipe is the same
as mom's diamond earrings,
which she gave to me in anticipation
of a future unnamable event
while holding a mouthful of air —
the cat saying grace over a mouse,
except here mom's life is the mouse.

Earrings
Written for Gina Blaurock, again, March 2025

When I did website work for her,
she paid me in earrings. Like I
needed earrings.

She's been gone 10 years now.
Too soon. More than usual, too soon.
We all say,

"She's here" when I wear them.
It turns out, I did
need those earrings.

More than usual.
She's here. Gone too soon.
We all say.

True Statements from Two Grandmothers about Two Grandsons

No matter how much you love them,
they wriggle free.
He is 90% struggle, 10% boy.
You should kick him out.

They wriggle free,
loose in the world.
You should kick him out.
He's a heart-attack in a glass,

loose in the world.
I love him.
He's a heart-attack in a glass.
He's definitely "in the family."

I love him
with my grandmother brain.
He's definitely "in the family."
I used to be strict

with my mother brain.
I call him my son's name sometimes.
I used to be strict
Now I'm strict like the river bank with a river.

I call him my son's name sometimes.
The river bank erodes, dropping pieces of its body into itself.
Now I'm strict like the river bank with a river.
And sometimes I'm searching, and sometimes I'm listening.

The river bank erodes, dropping pieces of its body into itself.
My own mother would have kicked him out.
And sometimes I'm searching, and sometimes I'm listening.
Ears, toes, face like mine.

My own mother would have kicked him out, she said to me:

I certainly wouldn't love and support that.
Ears, toes, face like mine.

I certainly will love and support him.

She said to me: I certainly wouldn't love and support that.
It's like I'm a ghost.
I certainly love and support him.
He can't even see me.

> They moved out of my house when he was a 1-year-old.
> I was a ghost.
> He cried all night in his new dark room.
> He didn't even see me.
> I knelt and rubbed his back, a back only as wide as my
> hand
> — I was a ghost already —
> until 2am when I had to leave.

He's 90% struggle, 10% boy.
He can't even see me,
no matter how much you love him.

When Your Body Is a Coffin

When your body is a coffin,
a mahogany box, shiny, rubbed
with lemon polish, it shows its whorls.
Hard now — used to be
soft. Sure, your toes are wooden too,
though still toe shaped.
Hands crossed
like a pirate flag.

When
your body is a wooden coffin, it
takes a long time
to fall apart, but
here we are. You did it.
Your body caught fire
and burned for decades,
knuckles, elbows, knees
crackling, askew.

Being a coffin,
you are and are not
like a tree.
Trees sever their limbs on purpose —
like you and that body of yours —
trees sever their limbs to stay alive
— your goal is the opposite.
Like we wouldn't notice.

That's the truth of it, now.
You rattle around in that thing,
knocking on the sides, brain withering
like an old nut. Congrats.

You burned so slowly,
what were we supposed to do?
Take you to court? That place
is made of kindling too.

You could have at least
lined the thing with satin flesh.
You could have at least
pretended to be sleeping.
We would have pretended to believe
you. Heck, we already do
try to pretend
what you're
wearing is more like
a hair coat or a dirty blanket.

One night you'll get up out of it
at last. Go for a swim.
Take the bus.

What Kind of Bug Do You Think That Is, I Start to Say But

I know it's a cicada,
big as a Sunday brooch,
wagging his thorax
for a few breaths
on the bleached sidewalk.
His rounded abdomen and
soap bubble wings
tick-tock around,
winding down.
And I say,

to the twins who are 4 years old
— like I don't know
about lifespans and rattling
bodies — like I didn't
see my father
in this very condition — I say,
how pretty he is.
So big.

Sex with a Painter, Lesson Number 1

I for one am surprised at how good
the words are; how the use
of the word "devour" sounds different

in the mouth of one who works with shapes
100% of the time. This mind,
these wrists

articulate like a camera,
distinguish between performance
and impulse. But also,

expression is not something to be taken
lightly. It never has been for me.
But that is, my expression,

even a thread of it slipping from my mouth
drops onto a welcome and willing canvas. Sure,
it's also splashed by both of us like a conversation

I've been having with myself for years
about a thousand shades of red (or, say, a warm blue)
and (turn the ship right the fuck now),

I come to find I am not having this
discussion alone — example:
what is that shine in your eye,

but something tight,
hungry, and
warm.

Happy Holidays from the Wet Ocean

I am celebrating Christmas
like I'm an iceberg that broke off,
from a bigger iceberg,
one you couldn't see the edge of
from the middle. Too bad
I often wished her ice to recede
— all winter, every winter, I'd want
that continent to get smaller. I'd
chip away at it when I could,
stomping on the edges of snow piles,
cracking pieces that got thin.
I didn't actually want her to go away. Now
not even a puddle is left and I am
celebrating Christmas like I didn't have
a big iceberg in the first place:
presents, food, kids, cinnamon
in the air, grass showing
on the ground.

Like the Movies

the stuffing
has been
dribbling out from

a jugular cut
in his giraffe
plushie

little puffs of
polyfil erupt
into the living room

pop up on
basement stairs front yard driveway
— a dervish galaxy also

like Andy Dufresne's
dust and rocks
I can check the toddler's

blankets
I can gut the beast
and refill it

sewing shut
its frayed
and beaming wound

we can start over

My Father's Desk

18 years after his death, it's here.
We lifted it out of the downstairs office—
comrade on a stretcher—

and loaded it (now in two,
three pieces) into my rattling car.
The wood smelled like

his casework, mom's Sinatra CDs,
and 30-year-old pictures. Also, all those
cigarettes. Also, when you open

a drawer, fresh teak.
Daylight liberator
from my non-writer

siblings, I carried it away from
the battlefield of our family
to three states away. Still a machine.

Wide planc. Gears. The drawers

puff out a soft cease-fire.
My brother's interrogation:

what did the house mean to me;
thank goodness
he didn't ask about this

because it already feels
like mine, my sweat blooming,
and my cold little heart — it beats

glee-
fully,
like it's charging the hill

that rises into the sun.
My comrade.

How to be a Witch

Be not special. Brew coffee.
Add cow's milk with a plastic spoon.
Sugar — same. Chant
prayers when you're young. Switch to poetry later.
Ride four cylinders.
Do this your whole life.
Sit with the kids. Make
a forest for the twins
to get lost in. Find them with a spell
your mother used to cast. Or mention
the dog and she appears
to lick their fingers.
Say this lizard's name
is "Skunk" and the one child
has a new friend. Snap.
Smoke. It all appears.

Infinity

Once I posted on my birthday
that I was still infinite

and another poet said, yes,
and another poet said, how

does that taste, and, cornered,
I had to admit it tastes like

dirt, of course red clay, of course
dark loam, of course sand

and bugs, of course it crunches like
sugar, it warms,

mist drying, it buzzes
like a collapsed vein with a needle

shining in the halogen light — never free me from this
— drag snap burn score scar —

I will step into it
every time, a surf,

the firmament, your body. I will.

Feeling Jealous and Sorry for Myself

Others linger on what they
inherited: the hair color, the fingernail
shape, bursitis and arthritis and

a tendency to wake up in the middle of the night.
Here I am with her diamond stud earrings,
and not a drop of her blood. The chicken recipes

I know, but I don't have
the smile, or the shaky singing voice.
I insist she's legit but others

say my real parents are elsewhere and
I grind my teeth, the teeth that
look nothing like her teeth.

Cathedral

Like a cathedral:
inside your mouth. The apex gives
it away, as high and rigid as a spine.
The arch of your foot; I catch your foot
in my hand like a fish. Your ribs,
cuddling as they do the lungs. When
you breathe out words, it's bellows
to the fireplace. The big walk-in fireplace.
Your skin does a great service
to the naves and fonts of your body.
Who doesn't love
the architecture and the vestments?
So many altars. Gospel. Song. Pulpit.
I should believe. Body. Voice. Mind. Mouth.

Advice from a Library

Actual advice librarians
have given:
"Shh."
"You can't do that here."
But also "Sure —
check out 50 books!"

And as I listen to the clunk
of a spine hitting the bottom
of the book drop, as I
spin through a digital work on Libby,
as I sail through the lobby
of the main branch,
the advice
the library itself gives me is:
We are all one.

This is old advice.

Lonely? There are crowds
in the metro to visit. Bored?
Jump on a pirate ship

I first heard it
with a shiver as a glib
and daydreaming young person,
but now —
as my parents leave me behind

and I am here
holding their empty, sweat-
perfumed clothes,
the library still says
keep reading
so I can smell someone else's dad's
short stiff, cigarette-stained whiskers
and taste someone else's candied
orange peels.

And the library bequeaths me
other days and nights,

food and furniture both,
wool clothes and sewn shoes. I have it.

As my friends disappear into closets
made by heart disease and cancer
— as they have gone from us
yelling or quiet as
a stopped pulse

the library says keep reading.
There's an anxious robot and its
spaceship friend gliding
through the coolness of space;
there's a soldier's story
told backwards.

It quiets
a crowded nighttime.

The library says
take this book,
its salt water and sugar,
leather and glue. Then bring it back.
We're in this together.

It rattles lights
better than any ghost. The library
squeaks old songs in key and out.
It speeds down the highway,
and stands in the sun
and hides against the scratch
of a brick wall.

That's what advice the library
gives me. Obvious, of course, it says,
keep reading. Certainly.

And you know, sometimes
it says something else: Sometimes,
it leans over and says,
"Write it down." Wind
and rain and bread and
steel. Write it down.

All the Math Is Gone

I went swimming for the first time since the day my mom died
and it was the saddest thing I've ever done.

My mother loved swimming and I love swimming
though I do laps, counting; she swanned back and forth.

Also since that day, the last time
I went swimming, I have been avoiding all of life's daily algebra.

And now I have gone swimming again,
and I could barely keep track, not a single

syllogism or formula or calculation
in my head and so I swan from side to side,

a pen, a cob, a motherless child.

Sex with a Painter, Lesson Number 5

Poets like to talk big. We like
to say we have memorized
the shape of our lover or

weighed the heft of them
by the mouthful. But a painter
actually does it, resting a hand

on the join, in back, at the top of your thigh
with the ability to make it again,
but this time as art.

A poet tells you it's art
and boom, they're done.
A painter, on the other hand,

looks at you, oil
pastel softening in the weather of a hand,
and swipes the same tension

that you have spent your lifetime
honing in your arms
across the canvas.

Poets steal all the time
— magpies and ravens all of us —
plucking shiny words

out of the air and gifting
them back like we thought
of them all by ourselves:

humid air rises and dumps
out a storm. Boom. I'm
not going to say painters never borrow,

never take, but I do know who makes
you imagine a thing
and who makes you see it.

Glass Blowing

We melt the glass first,
convert that which is slippery
into hot fluid. Then
add breath — all your breath.
Perhaps we meant to start slow.
You blow a zephyr
across hot coffee.
Perhaps we're lucky
that we both
would put our mouth on a burning tube.
Perhaps we're lucky
both of us spin the rod,
try, re-try.
Keep going.

Things That Didn't Happen

If she'd died twenty years ago,
that place would have been packed. In the hundreds.

As it was, there were 40 of us: a crowd
in one section of the church.

And each of us knew her
and so when I was writing

the eulogy we weren't allowed
to have at mass

there were so many stories
from as many points of view.

I had to whittle and pick and weigh.
Not the cantaloupe story because

it's the wrong kind of church,
not the celery story because that was for me, not

the pinch crabs because no one gets how funny it is
when your mom is behind the joke,

and so on until I was reminded of
when my brothers

were playing baseball (varsity, varsity, whatever, whatever);
she wrapped a ball in tape and affixed it

to a rope and swung it around her head
for batting practice because

there she was, her body turned into
armor, force, cadence, and target

all for us, swinging and swinging
right up until the neighbor kid
chipped her tooth.

On Nighttime

The sky is an o
pen mouth whiskey breath the skull
a galactic dome

o
whiskey skull drunk mouth
pour the sky into

these galaxy domes
so many brains they pen
the sky dusk and morning

buzz freeze
like day open up
pop a shot

throw it back
drink it down
water o

What Has Been Reported to Me
For Robert Tavani

To learn that, for one person,
my back is a meadow of freckles,
caught me by surprise. I
thought of myself for so long
as a trigger, a blur, a lost
chance.   And I lived that way,

like a beetle, patrolling,
ready for a fight. Now I imagine
butterflies will come to me
lured by petals and scent and I will
have to do something other
than wear this body like a 3-piece suit.

A meadow can lean and
bend and fill up
on sunlight. A meadow can
drink rain and harbor crickets.
A meadow can move
and be still at once, in concert.

I might not have steel hammers
for feet. I might not have an iron
helmet for a skull. We can sleep in
a bay made of sheets and puffs of breeze — this house
a creaking ship in storm and flat sea,
our bodies, our landscapes.

V. Refrain

How To Be Wrong About Something

Air in the summer rises
and we hide ourselves in our heads
and we become like smelly rounds of clover. Or rather,
we think we hide ourselves. We think we're unnoticed. We think we make
ourselves into nothing. We think we get more abstract all the time.

But I haven't ever seen one us with those kind of wings yet:
it takes a lot of time to learn to move like a wish.

And I spend too much time thinking about myself
and perhaps I follow others too much, tongue out.
Probably spattering the floor.

I hope there's medicine for it in the smells
of basil and rosemary and coriander
that go straight to the brain
and make me remember
every nighttime
when the nighttime was a box
and when the nighttime was a dome
and when the nighttime was a mouth.
I kiss your mouth like this,
like it's a bell ringing.

When the airplane dips,
pulling its fumes with it,
pulling some leaves on the ground,
I have trained myself to say thank you
for this kind of wakefulness
and the sound of scratching.

I have trained myself to remember
a few truths: everything has a quiet mode;
you have to breathe
someone else's air;
you have to drink someone
else's water.
This air comes from our delicate
heads, thin skin over thinning skulls.

When I think no one hears me,
when I am as good as a grave
in a conversation, I am (you are)
the sound of pouring liquid
right before it gets loud enough to hear.

We act like sleeping is a quiet activity,
washed of color.
But it leaves itself a residue.
We act like breathing is quiet too: a sealed face,
a mannequin, stealthiness, dog's breath.
But we are wrong.

Time Is Fiction

Here in the dome:
my unopened light sensors
tell me it's a little bit

morning out there and I
could force myself to sleep
again but instead ponder

the 31 years a horned toad
once spent entombed —
and he survived —

as well as the fact that we are
lucky to be anything at all
and luck is what I settle on,

my toes seeking the toes
of my partner: the fact
that here in   the dome

light   sleep   survive

ponder   seeking the fact
that we are   and   it's a little bit
          morning. Still.

Ritual

I stand at the sink, waterfall
coffee grounds into a strainer, and

cut an apple into ten slices on the wood
cutting board. All while

some kind of sun
flashlights into the room — glow, simmer, stare, mop

the floor with itself, or
implying itself as gently as possible.

I know people will miss me when I'm gone
then they'll forget

except for sometimes, in the morning
when the air thins

and the sun becomes a mouth, a moth, a goblet,
a swamp, a tree with tent caterpillars in its hair

— then they'll remember
because of how much I like this

routine, how it is
different every time.

For the Poets: Malediction/Benediction

This curse is for us who have
fished words from the mouths
of others, then proclaimed them mute. This curse
shifts, like we do, making the data
fit the conclusion, suggesting there's a truth
that's bigger than fact.
This curse is for the shiny mirror
we see in the world, mistaking
raindrops for introspection, mistaking
a cricket's song for approval.
Our role models: the jackdaw,
the cuckoo, the blue jay
who pluck gems, who abandon
love, who would eat the young
if it would get them a good story.
May we sing our good story
to the empty backyard
as sunshine glazes the house
as if it were the top of a mountain.

This is for us who curse
our mute mouths. This is for our
mirror mistakes, we sing them into
gems. We sing house into mountain.
We sing empty into approval.
We glaze. We eat sunshine. We sing.
We, crickets, raindrops made into facts. We, jackdaws
who make love bigger than the world.
We, cuckoos, mourn our good story,
proclaim ourselves fit. Curse us, love us:
we are plucked from a malediction.
We will eat the curses too,
having fished truth from data.
We do that
and our shine
shifts. May we see
ourselves in the world
like we do our songs.

Provenance

"The Apple Diet, A Timeline" was written for a group of poets who started meeting over Zoom during the pandemic called The Saturday Night Themed Poetry Exchange. Each week, there was a new theme or prompt. That particular week, the poem we turned in had to involve reptiles or snakes. And whenever I read this poem, I start by telling listeners this fact and that there is a snake in it, I promise.

"Canvas" was inspired by Rick Foreman, a regular at the Writers' Block Poetry Night in Columbus, Ohio, who was the real deal, "the essence," as Scott Woods would say, and the best at ending his every short poem by repeating a line. May he rest in peace.

"Fried Chicken, 1981" contains as much of the recipe for my mother's fried chicken as I've got.

"Tech Cycles" was written in conversation with Hypercube's performance for the series New Music at Short North Stage, February 6, 2024.

"To the Ball Python Who Lived in Our Dining Room" is based entirely on a true story and inspired by beloved Stir Fry, a ball python who had a sweetheart personality. But it was also partly inspired by a line in Scott Woods' barber shop poem about the kinds of sunrises and sunsets those plants know: they happen only "by the flick of a switch."

"My Manic Bitch" was written about Nova, a beloved dog.

"The Onerous Duty of Reading a Daily Poem Sent by Email" was inspired by and rejected by SWWIM, one of my favorite daily providers of a good (and sometimes great) poem by email. Don't worry, they did publish "My Manic Bitch" and sent it out by email on January 6, 2022.

"Divorce" was inspired by a poem by Su Flatt about an injured squirrel. Su reports that her poem was inspired by one of my writing prompts (about writing a poem in which you are not the good guy or hero). It is now Su's turn to write the next piece in this chain of inspiration.

"Made or Just Happened" — yes, the title is from The Adventures of Huckleberry Finn by Mark Twain.

"Water" — inspired by three entwining trees in my backyard.

"loved." was inspired by the December 18, 2019, podcast of Poetry Off the Shelf featuring a conversation between Timothy Liu and podcast host Helena de Groot, who discussed Linda Gregg's work. This is a great episode for many reasons, not the least of which is the idea of writing down six things every day. I'm citing it because Liu says "[If] you're gonna do the romantic love thing all the way in the way that the Sufis like Hafiz talked about it, then it's a different ballgame. You know, Hafiz was outrageous. He said if the beloved tells you to drink poison, you drink poison." And hearing that was the moment I had to write this poem.

"After" was written using a repeating line that is also featured in the poem "The Lie" by Su Flatt. I am sure I heard Su's poem before I wrote "After," but I forgot that she used this device, and I promise you, while they both use the same repeating word, these poems are very different and both worth reading.

"Ant" was inspired by the bug who kept me company one day on the way home from work and ran across my knee while I drove up the exit ramp of 670 East at 5th Avenue.

"Diminuendo al Niente" reminds us all to name our works of art something we can pronounce easily and with confidence.

"Self-Actualization" was written in conversation with Quince Ensemble's performance of their program "Dust to Dust" for New Music at Short North Stage, April 9, 2024.

"True Statements from Two Grandmothers about Two Grandsons" was written in conversation with the film Poetry screened at the Wexner February 15, 2024, as part of the Sonnets and Cinema series curated by

Scott Woods (who also wrote a new poem in response to the film). It is also the poem I'm working on in my author picture by Bob Tavani.

"She Looks Bored, You Say, of the Dog" is about a different beloved dog, Piper, and was inspired by Bob Tavani, whose words appear in the title. Yes, Bob is the painter.

"Benediction for a Cup of Coffee" was inspired by Rob Sturma's "Benediction for the Church of Common Sense," which Rob wrote after a poem by Mindy Nettiffee.

"For the Poets: Malediction/Benediction" started as just a curse for the poets but was expanded to include the benediction crafted from the words in the curse for the Saturday Night Themed Poetry Exchange.

Acknowledgements

Grantful acknowledgment is made to the publications where these poems or earlier versions of them first appeared:

"Celery" appeared in Clear Poetry

"Cathedral" appeared in Clear Poetry and in the Clear Poetry anthology.

"Fried Chicken, 1981" appeared in the Delmarva Review and was reprinted by Spy Community Media

"Tech Cycles" appeared in the digital chapbook Transformations and Actualization: Poems Written for the 11th Season of New Music at Short North Stage (2023-2024) created from the poems written and performed as Poet in Residence for New Music at Short North Stage 2022-2024

"My Manic Bitch" appeared as the poem of the day for SWWIM on January 6, 2022.

"Climate Change Elegy" appeared in the anthology I Thought I Heard A Cardinal Sing: Ohio's Appalachian Voices, edited by Kari Gunter-Seymour and nominated for the "Book of the Year" award by the Writers Conference of Northern Appalachia
"What Has Been Reported to Me" appeared in Cumberland Review

"On the Inadvisability of Good Decisions" appeared in the New Ohio Review (online)

"Twins" appeared in Gingerbread Ritual Literary Journal

"Snake Handler" appeared in Flypaper Magazine and received a Best of the Net nomination (2018)

"Sorry" appeared in the Laurel Review

"The Count Is Now 2 and Whatever" appeared in The Mantle and received a Pushcart nomination (2021)

"Ant" appeared in Slippery Elm

"Diminuendo al Niente" appeared in Open: Journal of Arts & Letters and received a Pushcart nomination (2018)

"Re-Piercing My Mother's Ears: the Plan" appeared in the digital chapbook Reflections and Reformations: Poems Written for the 10th Season of New Music at Short North Stage (2022-2023) created from the poems written and performed as Poet in Residence for New Music at Short North Stage 2022-2024

"Dear Second Love" appeared in Front Porch Review

"Benediction for a Cup of Coffee" appeared in Evening Street

"Canvas" appeared in After the Pause and received a Best of the Net nomination (2015)

"On the Delicate Task of Making a Password" appeared in Black Heart Magazine

"Self-Actualization" appeared in the digital chapbook Transformations and Actualization: Poems Written for the 11th Season of New Music at Short North Stage (2023-2024) created from the poems written and performed as Poet in Residence for New Music at Short North Stage 2022-2024 as well as becoming the libretto for the composition "it calls us home, and we go" by composer Rob McClure

"America" appeared in Willows Wept

"The Kidney" appeared in Dialogist

"What Kind of Bug Do You Think That Is, I Start to Say But" appeared in Apricity

"How to be a Witch" appeared in Loud Coffee Press

"After" appeared in the Delmarva Review

Thank Yous

This book would not have happened without my mother Joan Robertson and my partner Bob Tavani. The only way to love so much, so well, so hard is to have people who love you the same way. And that's how this book (and so much more) happened. Thank you for every minute.

But let's not be shy about it! I have so many more people to thank not least of all are my children Carrie and Andy Summerford; Jack and Zoe Johnstone (Sunday coffee friends and true believers in making art and making change); my writing group Mikelle Hickman-Romine, Sayuri Matsuura Ayers (who gave extra love and care, as she always does, with this manuscript), and Rikki Santer; my dearest friends including Scott Woods, Jesse Scrimager Galloway, Mandar Kathe, Vernell Bristow, Su Flatt, Zach Hannah, and Patricia Boughton; my publisher Bob Nelson who is always there to make things happen; and my twin sister Carolyn Bowen, friend from the start: she sees the best in people whether you like it or not and, as far as people go, she shines. Thank you all.

Portrait of the Author by Bob Tavani

About the Author

Body. Voice. Mind. Mouth. is Louise Robertson's second full length book of poetry. She is also the author of the science fiction novel *The Experiment Known as Rose Marie Hernandez Williamson* (Brick Cave Media, 2020).

Robertson served for 17 years on staff at the Writers' Block Poetry Night, wrote and performed for two years as Poet in Residence for New Music at Short North Stage, and earned numerous other honors.

She co-founded and is co-organizer of the Ohio MeatGrinder Poetry Slam and has moved her long-running prompt-based workshop series the MetaFactory online. (Look for monthly prompts at her Patreon: Patreon.com/LouiseRobertson.)

And here's the information you're really looking for when reading a bio: She lives in Columbus, OH with her partner Bob Tavani and their sweet, loving, wary, inimitable pets, Mari and Piper.

www.ingramcontent.com/pod-product-compliance
Lightning Source LLC
LaVergne TN
LVHW052033080426
835513LV00018B/2309